This Little While

FOR PARENTS EXPERIENCING THE DEATH
OF A STILLBORN BABY OR VERY YOUNG INFANT

By Joy and Dr. S.M. Johnson

By Joy and Dr. S.M. Johnson, Founders of the Centering Corporation, with sections
by Sherokee Ilse, Tom Golden, James Miller
and Rick Wheat

Revised 2016

Centering Corporation is a non-profit, bereavement resource center.

For additional copies and other grief resources contact:
Phone: 866-218-0101
Fax: 402-553-0507

E-mail: Centeringcorp@aol.com
Online catalog: www.centering.org

Forward *by Darcie D. Sims*

Many years ago as we faced our first bereaved Thanksgiving, I was worried. Our infant son had died in September and no one felt much like celebrating anything, let alone gathering family together to express our gratitude. Gratitude! About what???? What on earth did we have to be thankful for?

Our little guy had died after a horrible battle with a malignant brain tumor, leaving us exhausted physically, mentally, emotionally and financially. There was little to spend on a lavish meal, and I did not have the energy to even think about hosting a family gathering.

But, despite our unwillingness to participate in the passing of days, Thanksgiving did arrive and we did have a small family dinner. I think the turkey was dry, the mashed potatoes lumpy and I'm not sure we even had rolls. I set the table with our best crystal and china in a weak attempt at being "festive," but the only things that sparkled during that meal were our tears.

It is a tradition in our family to have the youngest at the table say the blessing, so it fell to our five-year-old daughter, Alicia, to find some words of thanksgiving. I was almost glad it wasn't my task to speak of gratitude when there simply wasn't any to be found around our table! How awful of me, a grown woman to wish such a job onto a five-year-old!

Alicia refused to accept her assignment. She refused in the manner of many five-year-olds and it became a battleground between mother and daughter, adult and child. She simply looked at me and said what all of us felt, *"What's there to be thankful for this year?"*

We argued intensely, and her refusal guaranteed the silence I dreaded. I knew this year's celebration would not be survivable. Her stormy face told me to forego the family blessing. We ate in grieving silence, each caught in our own web of stories, tears and sadness. About halfway through the meal, however, Alicia announced that she would say "something" at dessert. I wasn't sure what "something" meant, but I figured dessert was something to be thankful for!

As the pie was served, Allie told everyone to "hold hands like the Waltons." Slowly, awkwardly, painfully, we reached across our grief and clasped hands, forming a family circle around our table. Allie bowed her head, took a deep breath and in her five-year-old voice brought us the light.

"Thanks God, for this little while."

In our grief we had focused on what we had lost and worried about how we would survive another day. Alicia, with the wisdom reserved only for children, understood better than any adult around that table the gift her brother had given us and the gift for which we are forever grateful. . . this little while.

NOTE: Darcie D. Sims ©1999. Darcie Sims is author of many grief books such as ***If I Could Just See Hope, Footsteps Through Grief*** and ***Why are the Casseroles Always Tuna.***

Hearing the Bad News

It's hard to believe. Your baby has died. For many of you this will be the first experience you've had with grief, the first time you've planned a funeral, the first time you've said goodbye so soon.

If you have been handed this book in the hospital, read *Before You Leave The Hospital*, page 6, *Planning Our Baby's Funeral* on page 16 and if you have other children, *Your Other Children* on page 31. It's important that you make the most of the time you have with your baby -- this little while.

Shock and Disbelief

At first it's hard to believe.
You had great plans and hopes and dreams.
Now you feel numb and scared.
You may not know exactly what to do next.

It was really hard. The first thing we had to do was call the grandparents and tell them. There were some times on the phone when none of us could say anything because we were all crying.

Dad in Ohio

Making the sad calls is one step on your journey through grief. These are calls you didn't want to make; this is a journey you didn't want to take. On your journey you'll find yourself doing four tasks called "The Tasks of Grief."

You'll recognize the reality of the loss.
Grieve the loss.
Establish a new normal.
Reinvest in life and new relationships.

Recognizing the Reality of the Loss

I can still remember the shock and pain of sitting there 8 months pregnant as our doctor told us the baby I carried would die shortly after birth. How could he be sure? It must be a mistake. I refused to give up hope. Six more weeks I waited, prayed and grieved. Then came my labor, his delivery, a child born dying. I felt so hollow, empty and cheated of a future.

Denise Gleason, from our book ***Dear Parents***

Many times recognizing the reality of your loss begins in the hospital.

Your baby may have been stillborn.
Your baby may have died shortly after birth.
Your baby may have gone home for a short while.
But one thing is sure, just as we've said, this is. . .

Your Baby

Your baby does not belong to the hospital.
Your baby does not belong to the funeral home.
Your baby does not belong to the government. This is . . .

Your Baby

And the only time you will actively be a parent to your baby is in the hospital and throughout the period surrounding the funeral. Again, for this little while.

We knew the papers we signed in the hospital and at the funeral home would be the only papers we'd sign as Jordon's parents. These papers represented all our parenting of this precious child.

Mom in Omaha

See Your Baby

If you did not see your baby in the delivery room, you may be a little scared of looking now. While it's true that many babies have one or more deformities, we've found there is no such thing as an un-beautiful or frightening baby.

Your baby will be:
Carefully snuggled into a blanket.
Firm and cool to your touch.
Cared for carefully by the hospital staff.
Your baby will be your baby.

Years ago mothers were not allowed to see their stillborns. Doctors thought they were protecting us and saving us from suffering. It was as if they thought we would forget we were ever pregnant! Some women went to the store and carefully weighed melons or squash or whatever looked to be about the same weight as their baby. Then they took the squash or whatever home, wrapped it in a blanket and rocked it to see how their baby would have felt in their arms. And the doctors thought they were crazy. Pretty soon we learned it wasn't the women who were crazy, it was a society that denied them their motherhood - that's who was crazy!

Sixty-year-old grandmother

Hold Your Baby

Needless to say, if you absolutely do not want to see, touch or hold your baby you don't have to do so. Our advice comes from our years of working with both parents and hospital staff and knowing that if you don't see and hold now, you may not have another chance.

Again, this decision is up to you, but keep in mind that there are helpful staff at your hospital who have been there for dozens of other grieving parents and who know how to guide you through this early grief. They are there for you.

She was a beautiful baby girl and when her parents came to visitation I learned they had been offered a chance to see and hold her at the hospital and had declined. I told them she was beautiful and all they had to do was take a quick peek. They decided to do just that, one quick peek. The mom said how really beautiful she was. I explained how she would feel firm and cool and that they could hold her if they wanted to. They held her. In fact, they held her in the rocking chair during visitation. Everyone held her. Just before the funeral they came back, took her little casket into my garden, kissed their baby goodbye, said a few words to her as they put her in the casket and then they shut a little sunshine in with her.

Funeral Director in Ohio

As you go through this little while in the hospital you may be numb and somewhat in shock. This is a new road for you, and you've never seen the map before.

It can also be a special time.
It is the only time you will spend with this child.

It's very important to take your time!

As we said, this is the only time you will actively parent this child. You only have this little while.

If you want to hold your baby for an hour, you can.
If you want two hours, you can have them.
Other siblings may want to see and hold their baby.
If you want family members to hold the baby, they can.

This is your time. It is precious time. In many ways, it is sacred time, for it is the only time you have together, the time to begin to say goodbye.

Make Precious Memories

Take Pictures

They brought you for me to hold.
You were too small to be born today.
Your hands, feet and ears, so perfect in every way.

Your father and I shared dreams as one.
Would you be a daughter or a son?

You will never smell the flowers, hear the rain,
chase a toad or have a lot of fun.
You will never, never feel the sun.

From ***I Knew You For A Moment***
Pregnancy and Infant Loss Center

Your shock will fade, your numbness will disappear, but your memory of your baby and this little while together will last forever. To help you keep that memory, we encourage you to take pictures of your baby.

Pictures of babies and of adults who have died is an old and time-honored American custom. Before we began to be afraid of death, families took many pictures of their loved ones in their caskets or at home "laid out" in the old Victorian parlors. It was called Postmortem Photography. Relatives couldn't travel long distances in horse and buggy to attend funerals, so letters edged in black containing photographs were sent. Family members who could not attend the funeral had a written description of the final days, funeral service and photographs.

It was a really important picture for us. His little face was discolored and even a little out of focus. But his perfect little hand was holding the hand of his teddy bear. I came home and sat that picture on the table by our bed because it proved to the world that our little boy was real!

Dad in Michigan

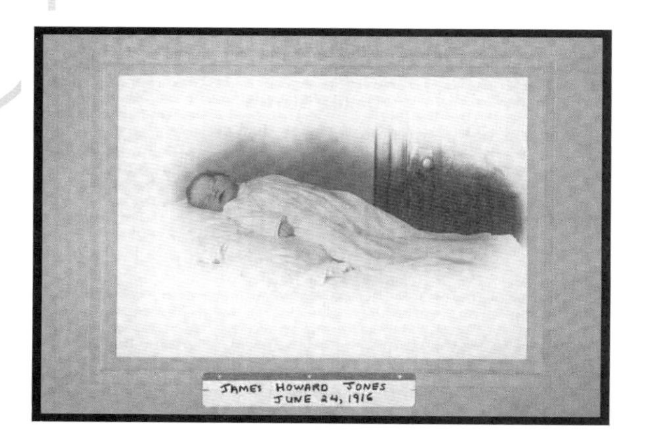

James Howard was a very large baby born to a very small mother in 1916. He died at birth and his grandmother suggested his picture be taken so his mother would know what he looked like and his family could remember him. This picture also helped his two subsequent sisters who have come to know him as the family remembered him through the years.

Theresa Vann, from ***A Most Important Picture***

When we began working with parents over 30 years ago, the standard equipment in hospitals was a Polaroid camera. It worked and still works, very well. Today, however, you have a lot of options. Mindy Gough, a photographer and counselor has these suggestions:

Photographic Techniques

If you use an digital camera or cell phone, you can see the results right away and talk about them. Make sure to take plenty of photos and back them up right away.

Use natural light if you can.
Place or hold your baby near a window.
Place the baby on a colored blanket.
If you have stuffed toys, put them in the picture.

You can use different zoom settings. This lets you take a picture of one tiny hand, a perfect little nose or ear or other small area. You can place the camera extremely close and capture the tiniest details. . .fuzzy hair, fine eyelashes and the like. A soft-focus filter makes your picture soft and hazy. There are many apps and new features you can use on your camera or cell phone to enhance and stylize your photos.

Someone on the hospital staff will help you and will be happy to take a family picture, as well. That way you can take photos of the family as well.

You can also make video clips of your precious time together. These may be important later for part of your healing process.

Telling Emily Goodbye

by Terry Morgan

Oh Emily, I apologize for what we did next. I apologize for telling the doctor I did not want Barbara to see you -- so she didn't. I apologize for declining the invitation to come to the nursery after your birth and look at you. I apologize that in a flawed world whose flaws we all share I refused to look on yours. I apologize for not holding you as if you were really ours, not some cast-off part of us. I apologize that we took no pictures as parents of newborns take to remember you. And I apologize for not being by you when you slipped from this world to the next where all apologizes are accepted and none necessary.

Most of all I apologize for not giving you the name that was yours, but telling them to call you "Baby Girl" on the certificates that marked your birth and death. We have since given you back your name...and made you real...and called you ours...and mourned your death...and even celebrated your life, dear Emily.

But we were on a road without maps and did not know the way to go or what to do.

Name Your Baby

Your baby was and still is an important part of your family. Your baby deserves a name and an identity. You knew and loved your baby before she was born, and you will love your baby until the day you, yourself die. When you name someone, you claim that person as your own.

Remember:

> Don't let anyone tell you you never knew this child!
> You know them well.
> You have given them their name.
> In many cultures, naming is a sacred act.

Keepsakes

In our culture, keepsakes, items which touched your baby during this little while are important, too.

I left the hospital in a wheelchair that squeaked
my stomach flabby with the baby-that-once-was
my face tear-streaked and pale, but I didn't leave empty handed
I didn't leave with nothing at all, I didn't leave all alone
a box on my lap cradled what was left of you
a hospital bracelet, a lock of hair, a stained blanket
soft tiny little ink-made footprints
and a card signed by nurses who still said
how pretty you were even though you were not alive
and on top of the box lay a rose from your daddy
no, I didn't leave empty handed, just empty.

Anonymous

Keepsakes of Our Baby

There are precious things to keep to remind you of your baby. Your nurses can help you get most of the items on this checklist.

Receiving blanket that held your baby
Cap and booties, if worn
Hospital bracelet
Footprints
Handprints
Earprints
Lock of hair, if your baby had hair
Birth Certificate, Death Certificate
Baptismal Certificate if Baby was baptized
Photographs
Monitoring tape
Record of weight, length, chest and head measurements
Tape measure used to take the measurements
Wash cloth used for bathing your baby

Not all hospitals do earprints, but it's exactly like printing the foot and hand. If you want them, ask.

Some clergy use tiny seashells to hold the baptismal water, others use parent's wedding rings. If you are of a religion which baptizes, you can ask for the container used.

Parents have bathed, talked to and rocked their babies while playing favorite music. All this helps make precious memories during this little while. Your staff will do the very best they can to help you get the items you want and do what you need to do.

They Really are Your Hospital Friends

Years ago we published a little coloring book called, *Hospital Friends* for children going into hospitals. The title is appropriate. You have a large group of caring people surrounding you for this little while.

Some of the women and men who work here have also suffered the death of a baby. They understand. Others have had special training. All of them can help. They can provide someone to listen to you who can also talk to you about the grief process and what to expect, contact any clergy you may want to see, give you books and other resources as well as keepsakes. They can help you find financial resources and information, give you time with your baby, inform you about autopsies and other procedures, and share information on physical care after you go home

People who share crisis become family. In some ways the nurses who cared for us seemed closer than some of my best friends.

Mom in Wisconsin

Your hospital friends can become close to you during this little while together. Some families have held services for their baby in the hospital chapel so they could say goodbye to and thank the staff, and so the staff could say goodbye to them and to their baby.

Before you leave the hospital you'll be told about taking care of yourself physically. You will also get information on such things as autopsies and organ donation. Ask questions! Your hospital staff is there to help and support you.

Planning Your Baby's Funeral

Some hospitals have a list of funeral homes and ethnic or religious communities they serve. If your family does not have a connection with a funeral home, make some calls. You can have a beautiful, meaningful service at a very low cost. Some funeral homes provide free or at-cost services for infants. And in general, funeral directors are most helpful. Here too, decisions must be made. You can consider:

Burial

There are tiny caskets, even for the smaller baby. In some cases, the little body can be buried at the foot of the grave of a beloved grandparent. If you want to visit the little grave and decorate it later on, choose a cemetery close to you. If you are going to bury your baby in a different location, you can transport the little body yourself. You will need a permit and death certificate if you are crossing state lines. Your funeral director will help get these for you.

I visited his grave every day for while, then it eased off. We still go there on the anniversary of his birth and death. We take a little toy and we have a picnic. I like doing that. It's a very calm and peaceful place for me.

Mom in Ohio

Cremation

If you choose cremation for your baby, you can also choose the little container which holds the ashes. It can be anything which can be securely sealed. Cremation also allows you to take your baby's ashes with you in case you move to a different city or area.

We picked out this little Peter Rabbit porcelain box. It was so cute and meant for jewelry and she was certainly our little jewel. It sits very quietly beside her picture now.

Mom in California

The Precious Goodbye

This is Your Service

It is usually not helpful to let someone else plan or take over the service planning. This little while is still yours to create and to remember always. You can have the service in the funeral home, the hospital chapel, place of worship, the baby's grave, or some favorite outdoor spot.

Take Your Time

It is possible to keep little bodies in good condition until family can get there or, if Mommy is still hospitalized, until she can be present. Some people will begin now to push you to hurry up and get over it. Don't listen to them. This is your little while. You will only do this once. Make it yours.

There are excellent books to help with baby's funerals, and you can get them sent to you quickly if your funeral home, hospital or a local support group doesn't have them.

I know of two memorable services in our chapel. For one, the baby's grandfather made the little casket. The other was conducted by the mother's uncle, who was a Catholic Monsignor. He dressed in his finest robes and you would have thought we were burying the Pope. Both were just wonderful.

Hospital Chaplain in Kentucky

Preparation

You can help bathe and dress your baby for the funeral service. The little body will be cool and firm, but not unpleasant to hold and move. If you had an autopsy on your baby, the funeral director may have put little undergarments on your baby to hide the incision. Remember the baby powder and baby lotion so you can have baby smells. If the funeral director is going to prepare the little body, make sure she or he uses them as well. Also put some powder on whatever blanket you chose to use.

The Visitation

The precious goodbye often begins with family and friends coming to the funeral home the evening before the service. This is the time when people come to be with you, meet your baby and share your sorrow. It is all right to hold your baby now and then during this time and if others want to hold your baby, this would be a good time for them to do so, too.

If you have never been to a visitation it can sound a bit frightening. In fact, it is often just the opposite. People hug you and you can cry together. You will also find you are smiling and sharing loving feelings. For many generations we have comforted each other this way.

I thought I didn't want to see anyone and I sure didn't want anyone to see ME! But I began talking. I found out one of my friends had lost a baby and at the end of the day I felt tired but really, really comforted.

Mom in Iowa

Make it pretty, make it real, make it baby -- that's what I said when the funeral director asked how we wanted our funeral to be. We wanted it pretty and real and meant for a baby.

There are many things you can do at a baby's service:

Read poetry - -from others or which you have written.
Write a letter to your baby and read it or have it read.
Write a letter that could be from your baby.
Play gentle music or nursery rhymes as people gather.
Blow bubbles as they leave.
Write your own prayer or psalm.
Create a naming ceremony.
Create a blessing of the parents ceremony.
Have a candle lighting.

If you want a clergy person to conduct your service and you don't have one, your funeral home can help find the right one for you.

Graveside

You can have a balloon release if you want. Family and friends can use markers to write notes on helium balloons and let them go, symbolizing the release of your love for your baby. We've found that balloons do not harm animals or the environment as once thought and are a beautiful sight when sent soaring together.

If it's above 60 degrees in the Spring or Summer, you can choose to have a butterfly release. While this is much more costly, it is quite beautiful. There are many butterfly farms listed online.

Grieving the Loss

Darcie Sims, who wrote our forward, also authored a book called, ***Why Are The Casseroles Always Tuna?*** You may have asked yourself that by now. After the funeral, when the burial is finished, the casseroles all eaten, when family and friends go home, your real grieving begins.

The following weeks I felt aimless, unable to focus and scattered. It was hard to go out. I felt transparent...as though everyone could see through me to my broken heart. It hurt to see a baby or a pregnant woman. I felt I should warn them what could happen. The urge to curl up and hide was almost overwhelming.

Denise Gleason, from our book ***Dear Parents***

Grief is the many feelings we have following a loss.
Mourning is the expression of those feelings.
You are likely to experience the following feelings:

Sadness

We cannot lose someone we love and not feel sad. It's an aching, a heaviness. You feel as if you're encased in plastic and can't reach out to anyone. There are times when you feel you'll never be happy again. You will, but for right now you'll have sadness and pain.

I wanted to yell, "You idiots! Don't you know a baby has died? How can you go on with your life as if nothing happened? How can you laugh when my world has stopped?"

Mom in Connecticut

Pain

By Sue Wolter

Sometimes grief comes and
knocks the breath right out of me.
It hurts so bad I can't think.
Moments go by...
Will I die? I wonder.
I'm not scared of dying anymore.
It can't be worse than this.

You don't break down when you cry, you break out in tears. It's a healthy release, a cleansing, a good thing, even if it happens when you don't expect it.

I would walk down the baby food aisle and cry. I would see a friend and cry. I would cry at my desk and in the car. I would watch a movie and cry. It took a long time before I realized this was something I couldn't control and I didn't need to control. When I had cried enough, I would stop on my own.

Mom in Maine

Another feeling that goes hand in hand with sadness is anger.

Anger

You have every right to be angry. Life isn't always fair, and this wasn't supposed to happen to you. You may take your anger out on your partner, your family, your friends and anyone in the medical community. God doesn't get off easy, either. As one mother said, I was so mad at God I didn't speak to him for a year!

Another found a different object for her anger: *I yelled at my other kids for nothing at all. I scolded my husband when he made any kind of remark. I kicked the tire on my car and hurt my toe, but the last straw was the dog. She hadn't done anything and I found myself yelling, really loud, Bad Dog! Bad Dog! and here were these huge brown eyes looking up at me and a little tail wagging. I sat down and started to cry, and she jumped on my lap.*

Tears and anger do the same thing. They both get us in touch with our emotions. When you are angry:

Hit the bed with a kitchen towel.
Write your anger into a journal.
Punch a pillow.
Take a walk.
Scream in the bathroom or yell in the shower.
Shout in the garage.
Break cheap dishes into a garbage can.
Talk and talk and talk to someone you trust.

Let your anger out in safe ways that don't hurt yourself or others.

Fear and Anxiety

C.S.Lewis, the famous writer said, *No one ever told me that grief felt so much like fear.*

When something bad happens it's frightening. Life isn't predictable any more. It is an uneasy time. Death has touched you and it's real. Not only do you fear for the lives of others you love, you are anxious about what is happening to you, especially if this is your first grief experience.

Know that most fears are unfounded and the anxiety, like the other emotions of grief, will fade over time. It may help to write your fears down. Make a list, then look it over. You're likely to see that your fears become less worrisome on paper.

Guilt

We are a people who want answers, and we want them right now! Often when a baby dies, the Why? questions are followed by the If Only's - If only I had . . . If only I could . . . I should have, ought to have.

Guilt comes with grief like rain comes from clouds. Again, write down your ought to's and should's and what if's. You'll probably see that almost all of them are unrealistic. As one mom said, *Guilt just isn't productive.*

Other Emotions

My favorite cartoon has two old women sitting on a bench by a pond and one says, "It's not good to wallow in self-pity, but it doesn't hurt to put your feet in and swish 'em around once in awhile."

Mom in Tennessee

In addition to the sadness, anger and guilt that come with grief, you're likely to feel:

Bad about what happened. (Why did this happen to you?)
Tired or fatigued (grief is hard work).
Restless, as if you're searching for something.
Forgetful (grief is preoccupying).
Lonely, abandoned and misunderstood.
Emotional. Many different feelings come at once.
Numb.

All these emotions, and more, are a normal part of grieving. Just knowing that they are normal helps you through those times when you think you're losing your mind. Feeling crazy is also a part of this process.

Remember that in those times when you feel as if you are in a dark cave, you're really in a tunnel.

A Flicker in the Darkness

By Marilyn Gryte, from our book ***Dear Parents***

Grief feels like a cave, an aimless groping
into a black, deepening void.
Into your hand I press the only candle I have
a message to flicker in the darkness of your soul:
Grief feels like a cave, but it is not a cave.
Grief is a tunnel, a journey.
The blackness is the same.
The only difference is Hope.

Physical Symptoms

Grief is physical, spiritual, mental and emotional. The feelings we've listed and which you experience are emotional. Your search for meaning in this little while you had with your baby is spiritual.

Reading this book, writing in a journal and making decisions about how you grieve and what you do to care for yourself is mental. Physical grief means we grieve through our bodies.

Your body is saying you had a baby. You did, and your body reminds you every day of your baby's death.

Some of the physical symptoms that go along with grief are fatigue, rapid heartbeat, deep sighing, aching arms, aching heart, headaches and sleeping too much or too little. You may have nightmares and vivid dreams. Your appetite may also be affected and you may eat for comfort or not eat because your stomach can't take it.

In the past, and even sometimes today, grief was treated like clinical depression. Of course you're depressed! Your baby died and depression is a part of the sadness of grief. Some doctors still want you to take anti-depressants, but unless it's a very mild sedative to help you sleep, remember:

Grief is not a pathological illness.
It's a part of life.

Healing Together - - Partners in Grief

Sharing our needs during a quiet moment.
Our lost dreams, our sadness,
our quiet hopes, our future.
We are changed, we are different,
but we are together in our new selves.
For now, we share a quiet moment.

The old saying that shared grief makes a couple closer is a myth. It will make you closer only if you decide it will and if you work at it. It doesn't happen naturally.

You loved your baby, and you will always remember your baby. Your baby would not want you to spend the rest of your life being sad, never enjoying yourselves, or breaking up because of this death. Your baby was an important part of your life, and the death will have as great an impact as the birth. What you do with it as a couple can help you grow and love each other even more.

Keep on "dating" even now:

Hold hands, go on a date, talk about how you fell in love.
Accept each other's limitations.
Both of you need support.
Your partner may not be the one to lean on right now.
Give each other room to grieve.
Stand close by to hug and listen when you are needed.
If there is a support group in your area, give it a try.
Avoid blaming each other.
Now is not a time to bring up old disagreements.
Don't accuse each other of loving your baby less.
Be patient.
Grief takes a long time. Slow down.
Now is not the time to make major decisions.

Talk about your baby and listen to each other.
In our culture, women tend to do more talking while men tend to work their grief out. Practice hearing what each of you is saying.

It's ok to not be sad all the time.
The first laughter after your baby dies often brings a pang of guilt. Remember, you honor your baby by laughing and living a full life.

Stay healthy.
It's hard to exercise at first, but it's a grief-reliever. If you can bike, hike or work out together, do! It's hard to be depressed when you're really exercising. Eat carefully and drink a lot of water.

Hold each other; love each other.

Love is cozy. It's the morning kiss,
snuggling into your arms before I get up, sleeping like spoons - your back warm to my front.
It's a smile, a tear, wrestling to the floor passion.
Love is you. Love is me. Love is us.

Let your first love-making after your baby's death be a soft and gentle stroking of each other. Some dread it because of physical and emotional pain and reminders or fear of the same thing happening all over again.

Love-making is communicating and comfort.
Let it be a time of joy during this period of sadness.

Accept your different styles of grieving.

Men and women grieve differently. Tom Golden, Jim Miller and Rick Wheat give us some hints in the next sections about the feminine and masculine modes of healing. The important thing to remember is that you love each other, you can heal together, and you'll both need space for your own grieving.

AN EMERGENCY PAGE FOR FATHERS

From ***Miscarriage: A Man's Book*** by Rick Wheat

If your wife or partner has just delivered a stillborn baby or your living baby has died, these are some things you can do:

Recognize the importance of this event. This may be the worst thing that has ever happened to the two of you.

She will grieve, and so will you. No one can lose anything or anyone of importance and not be sad, angry, depressed, anxious and more.

Be there! Don't let anyone, except your wife, tell you to wait outside, go away for awhile or come back later. Be beside her.

Allow her feelings and hold her. Let her cry, let her sob, let her scream if she wants. You don't have to try to make her feel better, just hold her.

Listen. Encourage her to talk about the baby and her feelings.

Share. You have feelings, too. Now is not the time to be the strong man and not cry. If you feel like crying, do. It shows you care.

Do something special. Get some flowers, a tender card, a small gift for her.

Be ready. This isn't going to end tomorrow. Grief lasts a long time.

We're All Different

The following two pages are from ***When A Man Faces Grief*** by Tom Golden and Jim Miller.

Often the types of healing our culture endorses are what are considered traditionally feminine ways characterized by talking about the loss, crying and sharing emotions with others. While these are good ways to heal, they are not the only ways. We believe masculine grievers have been too often misunderstood and unfairly judged simply because their approach has not been as commonly understood.

The purpose of any healing mode, masculine or feminine, is to give people a safe way to connect with their grief and pain. Many people find that the more commonly accepted feminine mode of talking about their pain provides a safe way to do this. This feminine mode is well known. It emphasizes interaction with intimate others, expressing emotions verbally and emoting freely. On the other hand, many men and those who grieve in the masculine style often don't find talking about their grief a particularly safe thing to do.

The masculine side prefers to connect.

The masculine side of healing is used by both men and women. It would be a mistake to say all men heal in one way and all women another. This is simply not so. The truth is that we all use both sides.

Learn the terrain.

When you have suffered a loss, especially one you didn't want or expect, chances are good you'll find yourself in unfamiliar territory.

A word many men use for their experience of loss is "chaos." What used to be dependable and orderly becomes unpredictable and confusing. It's a disturbing time. You're likely to feel ill-at-ease. Your stomach may get upset. Your head may ache. You may be "up" one minute and "down" the next and not have a clue as to how this happens, or why. You may become depressed, perhaps more than you ever have. You may get angrier than normal, either at other people or at yourself. You may blow up at little things in ways that surprise or embarrass you.

Determine your strength.
Grief is hard work. It depletes your energy and saps your spirit. It reduces your ability to concentrate. Grief lasts much longer than you expect and demands more than you think you have to give. What's the best way to deal with it? Let it into your life. Why? Because grief has an important purpose. It helps you heal. It allows you, in time, to feel better. It shows you how to grow with your loss rather than be diminished by it. If you do not grieve, you will not move forward.

Your Other Children

I'm so mixed up inside. I don't know what to think anymore. Sometimes I'm really mad at you. You left me! And I really wanted to be a big sister. Sometimes I'm guilty too. I wasn't with you when you left. Maybe I could have saved you.

Alicia Sims, ***Am I Still A Sister?***

We are often asked, *At what age should a child attend a funeral?* Our answer is:

As soon as a child is born.
Grief and mourning are love's sorrow.
We think a family who loves together grieves together.
We do not have a choice -- we will grieve.
Our choice is how we grieve.
Our choice is how we teach our children to grieve.
How they grieve their first loss will be part of other grief.

The wonderful thing about children is that they are not linear, they don't think in straight lines and with great logic. As Tony Sims, Darcie's husband and Allie's dad says, "*Kids are random access. They grieve then play then grieve then play." In between, they ask questions.*

Involving the Children

Preparing your other children and other children in your family to be a part of the saying goodbye is very important. Explain to the best of your ability how the baby died and how the baby will look and feel. Let them know that you will be there to answer any questions.

Explaining Death

It's not difficult to explain death to children clearly and gently, and no one can do it better than you. Older children will want to know details, younger ones just want something simple. Sharing your religious beliefs is helpful, too. You may want to start with:

When people die, all their body parts stop working. They don't feel or think anymore. They don't hurt. They don't breathe in and out.

They don't eat and they don't go to the bathroom. They are not sad or scared or happy. They have died.

Death is not at all like sleeping. When you sleep, all your parts work. You dream and wake up in the morning. A dead person never wakes up. The dead person's body will feel different, too. The body will feel cool and solid. It will feel a lot like the cover of this book. The body is like a peanut shell without the peanut or a schoolhouse without children. After you see the body, you may have more questions. I'll be there to help answer those questions.

Everything that lives must die at some time. Leaves die in Autumn and fall from the trees. Animals live awhile and then die. Usually people live a long, long time. Our baby wasn't healthy and strong like you. Our baby died and it was no one's fault. It especially wasn't anything you said, or did or thought that made our baby die. Our baby died because...

Age Appropriate Responses

Each child, like each adult, grieves differently and according to their own personality. However, children do have behavioral stages where some grief reactions may be common. Knowing these reactions can help us support and care for them.

Infants

More crying.
Thumb or finger sucking.
Senses anxiety, sorrow.

1-2 Years

May be clingy. Doesn't want parent to leave.
May sleep more. May wake more frequently.

3-5 Years

May be more "hyper".
Bedwetting is common.
Unable to verbalize feelings.
May ask questions.
Plays "death".
Reverts to "Baby Talk." May want bottle and diapers.

6-10 Years

Plays "death and funeral".
Shyness may increase.
Acting out may increase.
Grades may suffer. School may be a safe haven.

11-Teen

Anger is normal. Feelings that life is "unfair."
Acting out occurs. Philosophical talk with friends.
Search for spirituality.
Risky behavior is not uncommon.

What you can do

Infants

Keep to baby's schedule.
Keep baby in her own home with few visitors.
Talk to an infant as you hold them.

1-5 Years

Be honest. Answer questions.
Explain what death is.
Explain some feelings they may have.
Remind them that they did not cause the death.
Let them know they will be taken care of.
Involve them in the funeral.

6-9 Years

Be honest. Answer questions.
Explain some feelings they may have.
Talk about any fears they may have.
Involve them in the funeral or any memorial events.

10-Teens Years

Be honest. Answer questions.
Listen to some feelings they may have.
Provide them a journal to express themselves in.
Offer your love, understanding and support.
Involve them in the funeral and any memorial events.

Teens

Talk openly about feelings.
Encourage them to talk to a teacher or school counselor.
Create rituals of memory.
Let them tell you what they need.

Magical Thinking

Children often believe their thoughts cause things to happen. As Allie Sims says in the book, ***Am I Still A Sister?***,

Dear Austin: Have you ever heard of magic wishes? Once when I was little and you were littler, I wished you would go away forever. I sure didn't like you having all the attention. And then when you did go away forever I knew I had magic wishes. Please don't be mad at me, Brother. I was a lot younger then and it hurt me so much to have a sick brother. I didn't know what else to do. Hugs and Kisses, Alicia (former wisher).

You might want to say something such as, *"I know that some children believe what they think and feel can make bad things happen. I want you to know that nothing you thought, or wished, or felt had anything at all to do with our baby's dying. Our baby died because she wasn't strong and healthy like you. She just couldn't live. I want to make sure you don't think your thoughts or feelings or anything you did made her die."*

We never really outgrow our magical thinking.
Your thoughts about what you should have and could have done to save your baby are a lot like Allie's when she wrote to Austin that maybe if she had been there when he left she could have saved him.

It is important to let your other children know they are loved now just as they were before the death, and they will be loved into the future as you begin to create your *New Normal*.

Establishing A New Normal

You will never be the same person you once were. This baby has changed you, this death has changed you. What was once normal is different now. Your task now is to create a healthy *New Normal.*

It is a risk to attempt new beginnings. Yet the greater risk is for you to risk nothing. For there will be no further possibilities of learning and changing, of traveling upon the journey of life. You were strong to hold on. You will be stronger to go forward to new beginnings.

Rabbi Earl Grollman

Sherokee Ilse, one of the leaders in perinatal bereavement (infant loss) was first to coin the phrase, *New Normal*. It fits perfectly.

Your new normal may begin as you put away your baby's things. It is best if you do this yourself. Sometimes loving family and friends believe it will make it easier for you if they rush to your home and get everything out of sight. That's not true. Putting away never-used blankets and cute little outfits is a sad experience, but it also helps the tears come and is part of the goodbye. If someone has already done this for you, remember they did it in good faith and hoping to help.

It was as if your tiny presence has never visited my dreams. Everything was gone. Taken down. Put away. Vanished before my very eyes. Stored. Just as your memory is stored deep in my heart.

Betsy

A new normal is not a little while; it is a long time. It may be months before you really feel better, but in those months there will still be times of joy and laughter. You will never forget this baby, nor do you want to. There are many ways to remember and honor your baby. The best way of all, however, is to honor your baby by living a good life.

Ashley Prend, in her book ***Transcending Loss,*** says:

We can **SOAR**. We can accept and affirm our grief through:
Spirituality–looking for the meaning in our experience and how it can make us better persons
Opportunity–to help others beginning this journey
Attitude–it's true, we really can choose to be bitter or to be better
Reinvestment–developing our old relationships and loves and finding new, healthy ones.

To start your new normal and your reinvestment, you can memorialize and remember your baby. You can:

Plant a tree or flowering bush.
Create small plaques for your baby's name.
Donate in your baby's memory to a children's charity.
Arrange a space on a table or dresser for baby item.
Buy a special holiday ornament.
Have an anniversary birthday party.

I asked my five-year-old if it was okay with him if we baked a cake and released two balloons on what would have been our twins' birthday. He thought for a minute, smiled and nodded and said, "Yeah -- but we better make them angel food cake."

Mom in Des Moines

Reinvesting in Life and Relationships

Abraham Lincoln saw a beloved nation torn apart with war and his personal life torn apart with the deaths of three children; Edward, age 4; William, 11; and Thomas, who was 18. He wrote this:

In this sad world of ours, sorrow comes to all.
It comes with bitterest agony.
Perfect relief is not possible, except with time.

You cannot now realize that you will ever feel better.
And yet this is a mistake.
You are sure to be happy again.

To know this, which is certainly true,
Will make you become less miserable now.
I have experienced enough to know what I say.

"You are sure to be happy again," he said.

It is true.

Much of that happiness will depend on your support system, the people who love you and whom you love, and how you realize after the death of your baby, that life is very, very precious.

The Friendly Others

One of the challenges facing you after the death of your baby is the response of other people. Remember that most of the time people:

Are afraid of making you cry.
Don't know what to say but want to help you
Want you to feel better so they'll feel better.
May be afraid they'll say the wrong thing.
Do not intend to hurt you.
Are worried they will remind you of your sadness.

Many people think they know exactly the correct way to grieve the death of a baby. Often those who have all the answers have never experienced infant death or known deep sorrow.

Am I mourning the right way?
You know, I've never been the mother of a child that died.
So what are the rules?
Can I still laugh, smile? Should I feel so dead inside?
Do I cry too much? Do I cry enough?
What is the proper tone of voice?
I feel like I'm on display,
Everyone is staring and talking about me,
I feel like screaming, "Well, am I doing it right?"

By Sue Wolter

Many parents find that saying something such as, "I know you mean well. I'm just not at that place yet," helps. Others find that people they were sure would be there for them are afraid and stay away. At the same time, people you never thought of as friends come to you and share their own losses and offer tremendous support.

Your family may need some understanding from you now, too. Your parents are bereaved grandparents, not knowing quite how to help. Perhaps your mothers or aunts also experienced the death of a baby. They have a double loss in one sense: they experienced the death of a grandchild and they are experiencing your deep sadness as well.

I can't buy her an even better Jordan like I used to buy her a better doll when one broke. I can't tell her she'll get over it like I did when a boyfriend dumped her. I can't hold her and rock her and tuck her into bed and tell her it will all be all right in the morning. It won't. I can't take her hand and sit her down and give her instructions on how to do this grief thing. I can listen to her and I can dry her cheeks and I can hold her and hug her and talk about the baby and I can recognize that her loss is much greater than mine. And maybe, on some of the worst days we can be two women who walk to the corner and have an ice cream cone and cry together.

Grandmother in Maine

Unfortunately, you will often have the job of teaching people how to treat you, reminding them when you want to talk about your baby, letting them gently know when they say hurtful or unthinking things, and claiming your grief as your own. This is a time to take care of yourself, to cry without being ashamed or worrying about how other people feel. Ask for help when you need help, and give support to others as best you can.

There is no recipe, no list to tell you how to grieve or when to feel the many feelings that come. There is no map or outline. You have read about the feelings most people feel, the ways some families have remembered and the poems which flowed through mothers and fathers as they thought of their loss and their sorrow. Soon the time will come to reinvest in life and relationships. You already have one important relationship to remember and cherish: your baby.

Sherokee Ilse, in her beautiful book, ***Empty Arms***, says: One mother wisely stated that, "*Once I knew it was all right to admit to the pain and to know I would always love my daughter who had died, I started to feel better.*" You never have to stop loving your child.

Other people give the message, *"Now that it has been a year, you should be over it."* Let them know you still have bad times, but you also have good times. People who have experienced a death themselves often understand this.

There is no magic date, such as a one or ten year anniversary, when you feel instantly healed. It is a lifelong process. Most of the hurt will lessen, but there still will be days when you are overcome by sadness and pain. Allow that to happen.

When I first read this book I never thought I would feel better. I do believe that now, eight months later, I am well on my way to feeling recovered. There are many people and activities that are important to me. Now, many years later, I rarely feel the deep sadness and sorrow as in the early days. There are many times when I can hardly remember how devastated I felt at the time. It, too, has faded in my memory. My love for all my children brings me many smiles and much pride and only sometimes tears. Though their lives have been short, the gifts they each have given our whole family are immeasurable. For that we all are grateful.

You loved your baby for your baby's entire life. For many of you, you were with your baby for that whole short lifetime. That in itself is a gift. Your baby was very fortunate to have you as parents.

For Single Moms

For most of the book we have talked to you about couples. You, as a single mom, are equally important. You made the decision to have your baby, to love your baby and to do the best you could to give your precious baby a good life. Your sadness is different in that you face much of what we've talked about alone.

You are likely to have less support from people.
You are likely to hear that you are lucky this happened.
You are even likely to be told you loved this baby less.

If you are a teen mother, you may hear a massive sigh of relief from friends and family.

Whether you are 13 or 33, you will feel the emptiness and sadness and the intense emotions that come when a baby dies. You will face an additional challenge in comments from family and friends.

You may be angry at a society which doesn't support you in the same way it does married women–and even with married women, that support can be lacking when the child is a newborn.
You can be bitter about this, or you can see this as an important life experience, and you can be better because of it.

You owe it to your baby to grieve the loss, to take care of yourself physically and to honor your baby by living the best life possible. Talk to other single moms whose baby has died. Visit a counselor. Do everything you need to do to care for yourself. You deserve good care and a good life.

Caring for Yourself - for Mothers

There are four ways you need to care for yourself after you go home.

Physically
Emotionally
Spiritually
Mentally

You are reading this book. This and all the other books and resources you read or watch helps you heal mentally.

You will grieve, and after a time, heal emotionally.

Spiritually you may find yourself angry at God or drawing closer for strength. William Sloan Coffin, a noted writer, says, "The Bible doesn't promise a quick fix. It does promise unending support."

Physically you'll need to follow the instructions of your doctors and nurses. You also need to be aware of normal, natural hormonal changes. Get lots of additional rest and eat right!

When friends ask what they can do to help, say "Bring food." You may not feel like eating or you may want only comfort food. Force yourself to eat fruits and vegetables and take vitamins. Your prenatal ones are fine.

You'll get a list or be told of things to watch for. Be sure to call your doctor or nurse if any of these show up.

Going back to work can be both a relief and a stress. Your co-workers probably won't know what to say and will be afraid of "making you cry." It may help to talk to several of them. Thank them for their support, let them know you're going to be sad for awhile and that you like to (or don't want to) talk about your baby at this time

Our baby was a gift to us and a great teacher. We learned patience and compassion. We were given a crash course in values–things that once seemed so important all at once became meaningless.

There was a new depth to our souls, our beings, a learning, a wisdom, an understanding.

We would never be the same. We had made decisions of monumental importance. We had explained death to small children with wide eyes and eager, pointed questions.

We ourselves had touched death–death that came wrapped in a little blanket with lambs and bunnies on it. Death was not frightening; it was soft and smelled of baby powder.

We discovered friends we never knew. We discovered peop e we thought were friends were not. We learned we had to communicate with each other. We learned we were very different and exactly the same.

We learned how to let go and to go on. All these things were taught to us by a teacher who never spoke a word or taught a class and who weighed exactly 7 pounds and 2 ounces.

Dad in Arkansas

Sample Birth/Death Announcement

You can copy this message if you wish:

You were part of the caring circle of love which waited in wonder and excitement for this birth.

Now you are part of the caring circle of love which will embrace us in our sorrow, listen to us talk about our baby, and understand that something very important and something very sad has happened to us.

We are counting on your support. We hope you will share your tears with us, recognize our emptiness and continue to love us.

How softly
you came into our lives
But what a mark
your tiny footprints
have made
On our hearts

by Dorothy Ferguson, ***Little Footprints***

We have sad news to share

Our Baby
(line for name - leave another line for twins)
Was born at (time)
On (date)
And died at (time and date)

Moments, Moods or Memories

Moments, Moods or Memories

For more grief resources go to www.centering.org or visit our website: www.griefdigestmagazine.com for helpful articles on grief and loss.